HANDS-ON
HISTORY

Projects and Activities to Accompany

TALES AND TREASURES
OF CALIFORNIA'S MISSIONS

Randall A. Reinstedt's
History & Happenings of California Series

Ghost Town Publications
Carmel, California

Randall A. Reinstedt's
History & Happenings of California Series

Ghost Town Publications
P.O. Drawer 5998
Carmel, California 93921

Copyright 1993 by Randall A. Reinstedt

Contributors

We gratefully acknowledge the contributions of the following friends and educators in the preparation of this **Hands-On History** teacher resource book:

Cynthia Bergez, Teacher, Stuart Hall School for Boys, San Francisco
Kathy Nicholson, Librarian, Monterey Peninsula Unified School District
Ann Ostenso, Librarian, Monterey Peninsula Unified School District

Clipart images from CorelDraw 3.0 and WordPerfect® 5.1 for Windows™ were used in the preparation of this book.

Manufactured in the United States of America

ISBN 0-933818-64-5

10 9 8 7 6 5 4 3 2

Series Editor: John Bergez
Cover Illustration and Design: Ed Greco
Page layout and composition: Erick and Mary Ann Reinstedt

Contents

Teacher Talk

Welcome to **Hands-On History!** In this resource book you'll find a number of ideas for combining skills from across the curriculum as you explore the history and legacy of California's missions.

Although they can be used independently, these projects and activities build on the themes in Randy Reinstedt's *Tales and Treasures of California's Missions*. In Randy's accounts of mission lore, the missions are not just historical museums, but living links to California's past. In the same spirit, the activities in this resource book extend students' learning beyond the Mission Period and encourage them to link their own experiences and observations to their study of mission history. Besides learning mission facts and lore, students develop an appreciation of California's diverse heritage, explore the many meanings of the word "treasure," and play the part of historians traveling in a time machine to barter for priceless mission artifacts. They research and learn "facts," but they also practice important skills, such as working in cooperative teams and using scientific tables.

Thanks are due to a number of people who contributed directly or indirectly to the making of this book. In addition to the Contributors listed on the copyright page, Don Livermore (Monterey Peninsula Unified School District) developed a number of original ideas that continue to influence the **Hands-On History** series. The entire Ghost Town crew—Randy and Debbie Reinstedt, and Erick and Mary Ann Reinstedt—contributed ideas and suggestions, as well as improvements on everyone else's. Erick and Mary Ann wrestled the text and art into attractive page layouts, composed the type, and created illustrations; artist Ed Greco added the final touch with his exciting cover design and the illustrations that grace pages 4, 8 and 49.

Most of all, the **Hands-On History** teacher resource books take their inspiration from Randy Reinstedt and the love of history "as a story well told" that animates all the books in the **History & Happenings of California Series.**

John Bergez
Series Editor

We'd like to hear from you! We welcome ideas for projects and activities in future **Hands-On History** books, as well as suggestions for improvement. In addition, we invite you to send us photographs of projects completed by your students. With your written permission, we'll display them at our booth at conferences and conventions! You can reach us at Ghost Town Publications, P.O. Drawer 5998, Carmel, California 93921.

MISSION FACTS TABLE

#	Mission (in order of founding)	Date founded	Founder(s)	Miles from Mission San Diego (approx.)	Closest town or city	Mission Indians in 1832	Crops harvested in 1832 (in *fanegas*)	Number of livestock in 1832	Historic Highlights
1	San Diego de Alcala	July 16, 1769	Junipero Serra	0	San Diego	1,455	158,675	18,200	- First mission in Alta California - Rebuilt after being burned in Indian attack in 1775 - Named for St. Didacus of Alcala
2	San Carlos Borromeo (Carmel Mission)	June 3, 1770	Junipero Serra	440	Carmel	185	103,847	5,818	- Originally located in Monterey - Served as Serra's headquarters (Serra is buried here) - Named for St. Charles Borromeo
3	San Antonio de Padua	July 14, 1771	Junipero Serra	375	Jolon	640	84,933	17,491	- Noted for flour made by mission mill and for fine horses - Today the most remote mission, surrounded by military reservation - Named for St. Anthony of Padua
4	San Gabriel Arcangel	September 8, 1771	Padres Cambon and Somera (under direction of Junipero Serra)	105	San Gabriel	1,320	233,695	26,342	- Had the largest crops of any mission; especially famed for its grapes and winery - Partially destroyed by earthquake in 1812 - Named for St. Gabriel Archangel
5	San Luis Obispo	September 1, 1772	Junipero Serra	300	San Luis Obispo	231	128,751	8,822	- Located in "Valley of the Bears," where Spanish killed many bears for meat - Noted for its tiled roofs and woolen clothes made by Indians - Named for St. Louis, Bishop of Toulouse ("Obispo" means "Bishop")
6	San Francisco de Asis (Mission Dolores)	June 29, 1776	Francisco Palou (under direction of Junipero Serra)	550	San Francisco	204	67,117	9,518	- Built near stream Spanish called "Dolores" ("Sorrows") - Location near San Francisco Bay made mission a center for hide-and-tallow trade - Named for St. Francis of Assisi
7	San Juan de Capistrano	November 1, 1776	Junipero Serra	60	San Juan Capistrano	900	83,923	16,270	- Great stone church destroyed by earthquake in 1812, replaced by smaller church - Famous for swallows that are said to return every year on March 19 (St. Joseph's Day) - Named for St. John of Capistrano
8	Santa Clara de Asis	January 12, 1777	Padres de la Pena and Murguia (under direction of Junipero Serra)	535	Santa Clara	1,125	98,356	20,320	- Famous for its fruit orchards and garden - Used as college in 1800s; today part of Santa Clara University - Named for St. Clare of Assisi (a follower of St. Francis)
9	San Buenaventura	March 31, 1782	Junipero Serra	180	Ventura	668	135,303	7,616	- Last mission founded by Junipero Serra - Famous for its vegetable gardens, irrigated by canals - Named for St. "Good Fortune" (Buena-ventura)
10	Santa Barbara	December 4, 1786	Fermin Lasuen	210	Santa Barbara	628	151,143	5,707	- Known as the Queen of the Missions - Famous for the twin towers on its church and for the water system built by padres and Indians - Named for St. Barbara
11	La Purisima Concepcion	December 8, 1787	Fermin Lasuen	255	Lompoc	372	191,014	13,985	- Rebuilt after earthquake of 1812 - Scene of an Indian revolt in 1824 - Named in honor of the "Immaculate (Pure) Conception" (Purisima Concepcion)

MISSION FACTS TABLE

	Mission (in order of founding)	Date founded	Founder(s)	Miles from Mission San Diego (approx.)	Closest town or city	Mission Indians in 1832	Crops harvested in 1832 (in *fanegas*)	Number of livestock in 1832	Historic Highlights
12	Santa Cruz	August 28, 1791	Fermin Lasuen	500	Santa Cruz	284	58,072	9,236	- Located on north shore of Monterey Bay, some distance away from El Camino Real - Looted by people of Branciforte (a nearby pueblo) in 1818 - Named in honor of the "Holy Cross" (Santa Cruz)
13	Nuestra Senora de la Soledad	October 9, 1791	Fermin Lasuen	415	Soledad	339	68,408	12,508	- Epidemic here killed many Indians in 1802 - Severely damaged by floods in 1824, 1828 - Named in honor of "Our Lady of Solitude" (Nuestra Senora de la Soledad)
14	San Jose	June 11, 1797	Fermin Lasuen	555	San Jose	1,800	222,809	24,180	- Famous for Indian orchestra trained by Padre Duran - During Gold Rush, became a trading post for gold seekers who called it "Mission St. Joe" - Named for St. Joseph
15	San Juan Bautista	June 24, 1797	Fermin Lasuen	470	San Juan Bautista	916	69,577	12,333	- Original church was the largest in the mission chain - Famous for Indian choir trained by Padre Tapis - Named for St. John the Baptist (Bautista)
16	San Miguel Arcangel	July 25, 1797	Fermin Lasuen	335	San Miguel	658	105,049	12,970	- Famous for murals painted by Esteban Munras and Indians - Reed family used mission as home in 1840s; family murdered here in 1849 - Named for St. Michael the Archangel
17	San Fernando Rey	September 8, 1797	Fermin Lasuen	130	San Fernando	782	95,172	9,060	- Became a favorite stopping place for travelers, with largest dining room in mission chain - Scene of a small gold rush in 1843 - Named for St. Ferdinand, King of Spain
18	San Luis Rey	June 13, 1798	Fermin Lasuen	30	San Luis Rey	2,788	92,656	57,330	- Known as the King of the Missions; largest mission in Alta California - Famous for its fine wine and herds of cattle - Named for St. Louis, King of France
19	Santa Ines	September 17, 1804	Estevan Tapis	235	Solvang	360	179,725	9,360	- Famous for fine saddles made by Indians - In 1844 became site of first college in California - Named for St. Agnes
20	San Rafael Arcangel	December 14, 1817	Vicente Sarria	570	San Rafael	300	74,609	5,492	- Began as hospital for sick Indians of Mission San Francisco - Became full mission in 1823 - Named for St. Raphael Archangel
21	San Francisco de Solano	July 4, 1823	Jose Altimira	590	Sonoma	996	10,991	5,063	- The northernmost mission, founded to prevent Russians from moving south - Famous Bear Flag was raised near mission in 1846 - Named for St. Francis of Solano

Table Notes:

1. "Miles from Mission San Diego" refers to approximate miles along El Camino Real (The Royal Road) from Mission San Diego.
2. "Closest town or city" refers to present-day communities.
3. "Crops harvested in 1832" are measured in *fanegas*. A *fanega* was a Spanish unit of measure. One *fanega* equals 100 pounds.
   The crops included in this table are wheat, barley, corn, beans, peas, lentils, and garbanzos.
4. "Livestock in 1832" includes the total number of cattle, sheep, goats, pigs, horses, and mules. Some missions did not have goats and pigs.

Source Note: Data from The California Missions (Sunset, 1979); W. Beck and Y. Haase, Historical Atlas of California (University of Oklahoma Press, 1974); G. Faber and M. Lasagna, Whispers Along the Mission Trail (Magpie, 1986); G. Kuska and B. Linse, Live Again Our Mission Past (Arts Books, 1983).

San Francisco Solano

San Rafael Arcangel

SAN FRANCISCO

San Francisco de Asis

San Jose

Santa Clara de Asis

Santa Cruz

San Juan Bautista

Nuestra Senora de la Soledad

San Carlos Borromeo
del Rio Carmelo

San Antonio de Padua

San Miguel Arcangel

San Luis Obispo de Tolosa

Santa Barbara

La Purisima Concepcion

Santa Ines

San Buenaventura

San Fernando Rey de Espana

LOS ANGELES

San Juan Capistrano

San Luis Rey de Francia

San Gabriel Arcangel

SAN DIEGO

San Diego de Alcala

DISCOVERING CALIFORNIA'S MISSIONS

🔔 Table Talk

🔔 Mission Facts Treasure Hunt

🔔 Missions of California
Crossword Puzzle

🔔 Betcha-Can'ts

🔔 Why Was It Built There?

🔔 Related Readings

In this section students practice finding and manipulating information from tables and other resources—a key skill in many areas of the curriculum. Along the way they'll make a number of interesting discoveries about California's missions.

To get started, copy and distribute the **Mission Facts Table** *(pages 6-7) and the* **Table Talk** *activity. Then turn your students loose on the* **Mission Facts Treasure Hunt**. *Try dividing the class into teams to see which team can come up with the most "fact treasures" in the shortest time. (Will any team figure out that working cooperatively and dividing up the questions might help?)*

The **Missions of California Crossword Puzzle** *and the* **Betcha-Can'ts** *provide additional practice in using tables and reference sources.* **Why Was It Built There?** *introduces your students to map skills and geography while helping them understand why the missions are where they are. Finally, the* **Related Readings** *list gives suggestions for further exploration. By the end of this section, your students will be expert table users—and walking encyclopedias of California Mission lore!*

Teacher's Notes

Use this space to record your own notes about this section of activities.

Answers to Missions of California Crossword Puzzle (page 15)

¹S	A	N	F	R	²A	N	C	I	³S	C	O						⁴B		
A					N				A								U		
N					T				N				⁵S				E		⁶S
⁷M	I	S	S	I	O	N	S	O	F	C	A	⁸L	I	F	O	R	N	I	A
I					N				E			U			L		A		N
G					I				R			I			E		V		J
U			⁹B		O		¹⁰S		N		¹¹S	A	N	D	I	E	G	O	
E			A				A		A		R			A			N		S
L			U				N		N		E			D			T		E
	¹²R		T				T		D		Y						U		
¹³C	A	P	I	S	T	R	A	N	O		¹⁴L						R		
	F	🔔	S				B			¹⁵P	U	R	I	S	I	M	A		
¹⁶S	A	N	T	A	C	L	A	R	A		I								
	E		A				R			¹⁷S	A	N	T	A	C	R	U	Z	
	L			¹⁸I			B				O								
				N		¹⁹S	A	N	G	A	B	R	I	E	L				
				E			R				I								
			²⁰S	O	L	A	N	O		²¹S	A	N	C	A	R	L	O	S	
											P								
			²²J	U	N	I	P	E	R	O	S	E	R	R	A				

·10·

🔔 Using and
  constructing tables
🔔 Learning Mission
  facts
🔔 Cooperative
  learning

Table Talk

Do you know how to use tables? No, not the kind you put things on, but the kind you get information from. In science, social studies, and other subjects, tables help to organize information. If you know how to read and use tables, you can discover all kinds of interesting facts.

The Mission Facts Table is an example. Here are some basic tips for reading this table, and other tables, too. As you read these tips, try to answer the numbered questions. The answers are listed at the end of this activity—but don't look before you've tried to answer them yourself!

Table Tips

Tables are organized in *rows* and *columns. Rows* read across. In the Mission Facts Table, each mission has its own row.

1. Which mission is on the 7th row of the table?

_____

Columns read up and down. The *column headings* tell you what the information in each column means. For instance, the second column heading in the Mission Facts Table is "Date Founded." If you read *across* the 7th row and *down* from this heading, you will see the date when the 7th mission was established.

2. What is that date?

_____

Notice that reading *across a row* tells you *many facts* about *one mission*. Moving *up and down a column* gives you *one* kind of fact about *many missions*. This means that you can use the information in a column to make comparisons between missions. Try using the fourth column ("Miles from Mission San Diego") to answer this question:

3. Which mission is closer to Mission San Diego? (Check one.)

_____ Mission Santa Barbara   _____ Mission Santa Ines

continued...

With a little thinking, you can use tables to create your own comparisons and make new discoveries. Sometimes this can mean doing a little arithmetic. Here's an example:

4. How much closer to Mission San Diego is the mission you chose as your answer in question 3 than the mission you didn't choose?

_____ miles

Extension

As a class, or working in teams, create your own table of information and use it to make comparisons and other discoveries. Here are some ideas:

1. Decide what *kind* of thing you want to collect information about. An example is "students in this class." Each student would then get his or her own row in the table.

2. Decide what *categories of information* you want to collect. These will be your column headings. For instance, what would be interesting to know about the students in your class? The categories can include basic facts such as the city where the student was born, parents' nationality, or favorite hobby. They can also include things that can be counted, such as number of brothers and sisters, pets, or hours of TV watched per week. Here's a simplified example of what your table might look like:

Student	City of birth	Parents' nationality	Brothers and sisters	TV hours per week
Jamal A.	Fresno, CA	African-American	3	10
Kim E.	Seoul, Korea	Korean	2	15
John R.	Fresno, CA	French-American	0	18

3. When you've finished your table, brainstorm some questions you can answer from the information, and what kinds of comparisons you can make. For instance, how many different cities of birth are represented in your class? How many nationalities? What are the biggest and smallest family sizes in your class? How many students in your class watch fewer than 10 hours of TV per week? More than 20? What other questions can you answer by studying your table?

Mission Facts Treasure Hunt

Use the Mission Facts Table to dig up "fact treasures" about California's missions. The table has all the information you need to answer the following questions. You can find some of the answers just by figuring out where in the table to look. To answer other questions, you'll need to make comparisons and even do some arithmetic.

1. What were the first and last missions founded by Padre Junipero Serra?

First:_____

Last:_____

2. Did Serra found more missions than any other padre? (Check one.)

Yes: _____   No: _____
(Be prepared to explain your answer.)

3. What is the nearest town to Mission San Antonio de Padua?

_____

What is unusual about the location of this mission?

_____

_____

4. The padres celebrated a holy day called the "Feast of the Immaculate Conception" on December 8. Which mission was founded on this date?

_____

continued...

5. What tragic event happened at Mission San Miguel Arcangel in 1849?

_____

6. By September, 1804, a chain of 19 missions stretched from Mission San Diego to Mission San Francisco, far to the north. Thirteen years went by before a 20th mission was added. What was this mission?

_____

Why was it founded?

_____

7. Six years later, the last California mission was founded. Why did the padres add this 21st mission to the chain?

_____

_____

8. Which mission had the fewest mission Indians in 1832? How many more Indians would this mission need to catch up to the mission with the next smallest number of Indians?

Which: _____   How many: _____

9. In 1832 only one mission ranked first among all the missions in _more than one_ category (mission Indians, crops, or livestock). What prosperous mission was this?

_____

In which categories did it rank first?

_____

10. Two northern California missions, San Francisco and Santa Clara, were founded within less than a year of each other. By 1832, which of these two missions would you say was larger and richer? (Be prepared to explain your answer.)

_____

_____

- Language skills
- Using tables
- Problem solving

Missions of California Crossword Puzzle

The puzzle on this page includes some part of the name of each of California's 21 missions. Can you fill in the missing parts of each name? Here are some hints:

1. **All the clues refer to information in the Mission Facts Table. Use the table to figure out which mission is being named.**
2. **The number of each clue (Across or Down) tells you where to begin writing the answer. Notice that #7 Across and #4 Down are already filled in for you.**
3. **The number of squares for each clue tells you how many letters are missing. Use this number as a hint to find the answer.**
4. **Sometimes the missing part of the mission name contains more than one word. There is no space between words in the finished puzzle. (See how the answer is written for #7 Across.)**
5. **Wherever an Across word crosses a Down word, the two words share the same letter.**
6. **You can skip around and solve the easiest clues first. Sometimes shared letters will help you fill in a missing word.**

MISSIONS OF CALIFORNIA CROSSWORD PUZZLE CLUES

Across

1. Mission _____ de Asis is also known as Mission Dolores, after the Spanish name of a nearby stream.

7. The subject of this puzzle.

11. The founding of Mission _____ in July, 1769, marked the beginning of California's famed mission chain.

13. Located about 60 miles from #11 Across, Mission San Juan de _____ is famous for its swallows.

15. Located near the present-day town of Lompoc, La _____ Concepcion was named in honor of the "Immaculate Conception."

16. Like #1 Across, Mission _____ de Asis is named for a saint from the Italian town of Assisi. Today this mission is part of a university campus.

17. The name of Mission _____ , one of two missions founded in 1791, means "Holy Cross."

19. Mission _____ Arcangel had the largest crops of any mission (more than 200,000 *fanegas* were harvested there in 1832).

20. The famous Bear Flag revolt in 1846 took place near the last and northernmost mission, Mission San Francisco de _____ .

21. Also known as Carmel Mission, Mission _____ Borromeo became Junipero Serra's headquarters and final resting place.

22. Padre _____ is buried at #21 Across.

Down

1. One of four missions established by Padre Fermin Lasuen in 1797, Mission _____ Arcangel is famous for the murals painted by Esteban Munras and Indian artists.

2. Founded about a year after #21 Across, Mission San _____ de Padua is today surrounded by a military reservation.

3. The last of the four missions established in 1797, Mission _____ Rey was the scene of a small gold rush in 1843.

4. The last mission founded by Junipero Serra, Mission San _____ is named for "Saint Good Fortune."

5. Named for "Our Lady of Solitude," Nuestra Senora de la _____ was the scene of a tragic epidemic that killed many Indians in 1802.

6. The first of the four missions established in 1797, Mission _____ became known to goldseekers as "Mission St. Joe" during the Gold Rush.

8. The second of two missions named for kings, Mission San _____ became known as the King of the Missions because of its size.

9. Named for St. John the Baptist, Mission San Juan _____ boasted the largest church in the mission chain.

10. Known as the Queen of the Missions, Mission _____ was the first mission founded by Padre Fermin Lasuen.

12. Founded by Padre Vicente Sarria, Mission San _____ Arcangel began as a hospital outpost of #1 Across.

14. Located in the "Valley of the Bears," Mission San _____ was founded almost exactly a year after #19 Across.

18. Founded by Padre Estevan Tapis, Mission Santa _____ became famous for the fine saddles made by the mission Indians.

Teacher's Note: The completed puzzle is found on page 10.

- Cooperative learning
- Problem solving
- Math skills
- Geography and map skills
- Using tables
- Research skills

Can you or your team score 100 points? Betchacan't!

Betcha-Can'ts

Finding the answers to the following questions about California's missions may involve a little research. The information in the Mission Facts Table will help—but you won't be able to stop there! You may also need to hunt in atlases, encyclopedias, or other reference books.

Each answer is worth the number of points shown. How many points can you score?

1. OK, here's an easy one to start with—if you have your Mission Facts Table handy. In 1976, the United States celebrated the 200th anniversary of the signing of the Declaration of Independence. Which two California missions also celebrated their 200th birthdays that year? **(5 points)** Got that one already? All right, then, how many missions are *older* than the Declaration of Independence? (Careful! Don't forget the one that was "born" just a few days before the declaration was signed.) **(5 points)**

2. The special year 1997 marks the 200th birthday of four California missions. No, I don't want you to tell me which ones. I want to know which of these four missions is *closest* to your community (just in case you feel like joining the celebration!). **(5 points)** Wait, that's not all . . . About how many air miles is it from that mission to your community? (Hmm . . . How will you figure this one out? Maybe a California map and a ruler would help . . . OK, here's another hint: If you can't find the missions on a map of California, try locating their nearest town or city, as shown in the Mission Facts Table. Then you can measure from there.) **(5 points)**

3. Now try this one on for size: In what year will the *last* mission founded in California celebrate its 200th birthday? And, just for fun, how old will *you* be in that year? **(5 points)**

4. Padre Fermin Lasuen chose the location for Mission Soledad in 1791 partly because it nicely filled in the mission chain. From Soledad, it was about "a day's

continued...

walk" to either Mission San Carlos *or* Mission San Antonio. Based on this information, about how many miles did the padres think was "a day's walk"—was it closer to (a) 10, (b) 30, or (c) 50 miles? (Better get that map out again!) **(10 points)**

5. Speaking of sore feet, on several occasions Padre Junipero Serra walked all the way from his headquarters at Mission San Carlos to Mission San Diego, and back again. (Whew! And he was around 60 years old at the time!) So, about how far did Serra walk on one round trip? (Hey, this is easy—if you check the distances in the Mission Facts Table.) **(5 points)** Now that you know how many miles he walked, let's see if you can figure out how long it took him. If Serra walked 25 miles per day, about how many days would it take him to make the round trip between Missions San Carlos and San Diego? **(5 points)**

6. If Padre Serra were alive today, he could rest his feet and take a car on his journeys from mission to mission. Suppose he drove the same number of miles as he walked in question 5. At a speed of 50 miles per hour, how long would it take him to make the round trip? **(5 points)**

7. Several Spanish words can be learned from the names of the missions. Using the Mission Facts Table, can you figure out the Spanish word that means (a) "saint" (male); (b) "saint" (female); (c) "king"; and (d) "of"? **(5 points** each, for a whopping **20 points!**)

8. While we're on the subject of names . . . The name of a large national forest in California has something to do with the people who founded the missions. Can you find the name of this national forest? (Hint: The forest has portions in both southern and central California.) **(5 points)** Wait, don't put the atlas away yet! The northern part of this forest has a mountain peak named for a rather famous person connected with the missions. What is the name of this peak? (Give up? Try looking west of King City.) **(5 points)**

9. I know you're gonna hate this one . . . To measure the weight of their crops, the Spanish used a unit called a *fanega*. One *fanega* equals 100 pounds. At Mission San Juan Capistrano in 1832, there were about 93 *fanegas* of crops harvested for every Indian at the mission. About how many pounds of crops is that per Indian? **(5 points)** Gee, I guess they worked hard, huh? Now, for another 5 points, can you figure out what that amount is in tons? (If you're not sure how many pounds are in a ton, where should you look for the answer?) **(5 points)**

10. Did you really get this far? All right, you asked for it . . . In 1812, several missions in southern California were damaged by an earthquake. Some years later, the strongest earthquake ever recorded in California also happened in the southern part of the state. Betchacan't find out (a) how many years after 1812 California's strongest-ever quake occurred and (b) where it was centered! **(10 points)**

PERFECT SCORE: 100   YOUR SCORE: _____

Why Was It Built There?

The missions were built in the locations they were for many reasons. Some of those reasons were just like the reasons you live where you do today. The Spanish needed water, food, a good climate, and an easy way to get to the location. There were other reasons, too. The padres who built the missions eventually wanted a chain of missions a "day's walk" apart so that a person could walk from one to another. They wanted locations that would allow them to make contact with friendly Indians. They also wanted to be as close to the coast as possible, preferably near a protected harbor, to establish the Spanish presence and discourage other countries from occupying the land (including the Russians who were moving down the coast hunting furs). There were a lot of other reasons the missions were built in the locations they were. The reasons listed above will help you begin to understand them.

Directions _____

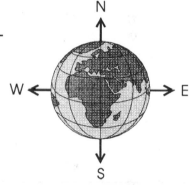

1. Study the map of the imaginary land. Use the legend to understand the symbols on the map.

2. You are a padre whose job it is to place 5 missions in the area on the map. Keep in mind the guidelines below:

- A mission should be **near the coast** if possible (establishes a Spanish presence and supply point).
- The missons should be approximately **"a day's walk" apart** (let's say from 20 to 30 miles) and easy to get to.
- A mission needs **fresh water** (salt water doesn't count).
- There should be a **moderate climate** (good weather means that crops can grow, animals can live, and people are comfortable).

3. Label your missions A, B, C, D, and E. On a separate piece of paper explain why you chose the locations you did for each of your missions. Refer to the guidelines above (#2), and any other items you think are important. Remember, this is an imaginary map of an imaginary land. Your goal here is to better understand the *type* of things the padres had to consider when planning and building their missions. You are lucky, you have a map! The padres had to rely on information from others (friendly Indians, early explorers, etc.). Then they had to travel through potentially dangerous land to find the best locations.

Hint: If you want to easily figure out how far 30 miles is on the map when you are not traveling in a perfectly straight line, cut a piece of string to the length that represents 30 miles by laying it next to the scale on the map. Then you can lay the string along any route you want and it will represent 30 miles.

Teacher's Instructions _____

1. Copy and distribute the activity page (page 19) and the map (page 20).

2. Go over the *legend* with students to be sure they understand the meanings of the symbols. Emphasize these points about the physical features of the Land of Opportunity:

a. Students can assume that rivers can be crossed.
b. Mountains can *not* be crossed; travelers must walk around them (adding miles to the journey).
c. Where mountains go all the way to the coast, travelers must go inland to get around them.

3. When presenting this activity, and in evaluating students' work, remember that there is no single set of right answers. However, there are wrong answers. Emphasize that what is important is the students' *explanations* of why they chose the locations they did. Did they take all the guidelines into consideration? If not, why not? What other elements did they consider when placing their missions? If they picked a location that did not have all the essentials for survival (fresh water, food, etc.), what would have to be done to make up for the missing elements? How far could they expect someone to walk for food and fresh water? How would they transport the water? If they chose to build within range of "dangerous animals," what precautions would they have to take to keep the inhabitants safe? What weapons were available during the Mission Period?

4. In addition to plotting the locations of the missions, students can also color their maps. You may want to include the finished maps in a "California Missions" bulletin board, or in a display that you make out of your students' completed projects and activities from this book.

Extensions _____

Geography has always played a major role in people's movements and lifestyles, from driving to grandmother's house to going to war over natural resources or transportation routes. **Why Was It Built There?** opens a myriad of possibilities for pursuing a deeper discussion of the important impact of geography in both history and current events. Put on your creative thinking cap, and let the following ideas spark your imagination!

Understanding the King's Highway

Use the activity to probe further into the subject of **why El Camino Real's route took the shape it did, and why the missions were built in the locations they were.**

1. Have your students divide reasons for the missions' locations into *physical geography reasons* and *other reasons*. Discuss each reason. Do they still apply to people today? What might a modern day example be? Some *physical geography reasons* include the presence of timber, the accessibility of the region to moderate walkers (e.g., the locations

continued...

of mountain passes and river crossings), fresh water sources, soil capable of supporting crops, tolerable climate, and protected harbors.

Some *other reasons* include the desire to build a chain of missions "a day's walk" apart, the desire to use the missions to assert a presence along the coast, the abundance of game, and the location of friendly or unfriendly California Indians.

Some of the *other reasons* for the missions' locations fall into areas of *non-physical geography,* which includes *cultural geography, political geography,* and *historical geography.* These aspects of geography are linked together, and change in one affects the others. The actions of individuals and nations are often driven by geographical factors. Many books have been written on the subject of geography in general, as well as its various aspects. With a little research, combined with your creativity in relating the information to your students, you can develop material that will spark hours of classroom discussion, and allow your students to better understand the world around them. . . past, present, and future.

2. Study El Camino Real at various levels. You can map the entire mission chain and study it as a region, analyzing climate, mountain ranges and passes, distances between missions, proximity to the coast, and so on. You can also study El Camino Real at a much closer level. Divide the class into groups and have each group study an individual mission location, analyzing the pros and cons of the site. To do this, you'll need a detailed atlas or map showing the physical features of the area around the mission. (If such items are unavailable at your school, try sporting-goods or mountaineering stores, government agencies, or the Chambers of Commerce located near the missions. A topographical map is best.)

Beyond El Camino . . .

1. Use this activity to reinforce students' understanding of maps, map legends, scales, and geographic concepts such as north and south. Start with a world map and work your way down to maps showing the nation, state, county, and city or town. Point out how detail is gained as smaller areas are covered. Discuss the similarities and differences between maps drawn on different scales. Have students draw a map of their route to school that includes symbols, compass direction, and a legend.

2. Discuss current events from a geographical perspective. The daily news can provide any number of topics for discussion of physical, cultural, political, and historical geography. For instance, several times in California history, there have been moves to divide the state into two or more smaller states. What are some of the reasons for these proposals? Where have people suggested drawing the new state boundaries, and why? What part does water play in California's politics and living patterns (what made it possible for so many people to move to southern California?)? On the national and international levels, what physical features and historical causes contribute to the shape of the United States (for instance, where the boundary is drawn with Mexico)? How does geography help us understand issues such as the problem of illegal immigrants crossing the border to find work? Why are our cities so overpopulated, while large portions of our country have so much wide-open land? Why is the Panama Canal so important? Once you start thinking in geographical terms, the possibilities are endless!

Related Readings

This resource list includes stories suitable for fourth graders, nonfiction sources, activity-oriented publications, and books that teachers will find useful for background information and illustrations.

Anderson, Joan. SPANISH PIONEERS OF THE SOUTHWEST. *With photos by George Ancona at Golondrias (near Santa Fe, New Mexico), and the help of the village interpreters, readers will get an idea of what life was like for the Spanish settlers of the mid-1700s.*

Bauer, Helen. CALIFORNIA MISSION DAYS. *This former state textbook describes each mission's settlement, growth, and decay; the interesting text is embellished by authentic "then and now" illustrations.*

CALIFORNIA MISSIONS: THE EARLIEST SERIES OF VIEWS. (Bellerophon Books.) *Taken from the journal and drawings of Henry Miller, this book provides an inexpensive view of the missions in 1856, prior to their decay. (Teacher's resource.)*

CALIFORNIA'S PAST. (Conceptual Productions.) *This book contains several mission activities, including Mission Floor Plan; Mission Scramble (vocabulary); Mission Life (story starters); Find the Missions (word scramble); and a "You Are There" interview format.*

Coerr, Eleanor. THE BELL RINGER AND THE PIRATES. *Based on a true story of Mission San Juan Capistrano, this easy-to-read book tells of a young Ahachmai Indian boy who warns the mission people of the coming of privateer Hippolyte de Bouchard and his gang in 1818.*

Dolan, Sean. JUNIPERO SERRA. *This illustrated biography was created to present a balanced view of Serra and the effect of European settlement on California's Indians. (Teacher's resource; may be suitable for advanced readers.)*

Faber, Gail, and Michele Lasagna. PASQUALA: THE STORY OF A CALIFORNIA INDIAN GIRL. *Set near Mission Santa Ines, this story explores the conflict between California Indian culture and the mission system.*

Faber, Gail, and Michele Lasagna. WHISPERS ALONG THE MISSION TRAIL. *Written as a text, this lavishly illustrated book explores many aspects of mission life and provides a broad overview of California's early explorers and settlers.*

continued...

Garthwaite, Marion. TOMAS AND THE RED-HEADED ANGEL. *In this story of the early rancho period, Angelita, the niece of one of the ranchers, is faced with a marriage arranged by her father. She persuades Tomas, a young Indian boy, to help her escape and elope with another.*

Grap, Genevieve. HOW FAR, FELIPE? *Felipe and his family travel hundreds of miles from Mexico with Colonel Anza to settle Alta California.*

Kuska, George, and Barbara Linse. LIVE AGAIN OUR MISSION PAST. *This book is full of activities, recipes, time lines, stories, history, games, craft projects, and more. The authors invite teachers to photocopy anything in the book for distribution in the classroom.* (Teacher's resource; also suitable for students to consult on their own.)

Martin, Carol O. EXPLORING THE CALIFORNIA MISSIONS: ACTIVITY CARDS. *This collection of bound activity cards provides basic facts and build-to-scale activities for each mission, together with a number of activities that develop skills in math, writing, geography, research, and other areas.* (Teacher's resource.)

Neuerburg, Norman. THE DECORATION OF THE CALIFORNIA MISSIONS. *This Bellerophon Book explores the colorful designs and architectural features that decorated both the interior and the exterior of California's missions; an excellent resource for integrating art study and activities into the exploration of the Mission Period.*

O'Dell, Scott. ZIA. *A young Indian girl moves to Mission Santa Barbara to be close to the island her aunt Karana is living on. The descriptive text gives readers a good idea of mission life from the Indians' point of view.*

Politi, Leo. THE MISSION BELL. *This short biography tells the story of Padre Serra's journey to California to establish missions as a haven for the California Indians and the Spaniards alike.*

Politi, Leo. SONG OF THE SWALLOWS. *A young boy befriends the old gardener at Mission San Juan Capistrano, learns about the early days of the mission, and helps ring the bells to welcome back the swallows on St. Joseph's Day.*

Roberts, Helen M. MISSION TALES. (Seven volumes.) *Each volume in this set features three missions and tells what life was like at each, including the padres' efforts to convert the California Indians and the resistance they encountered.*

Roberts, Margaret. PIONEER CALIFORNIA. *This is a collection of tales of explorers, California Indians, and settlers; includes an excellent bibliography.*

Young, Stanley. THE MISSIONS OF CALIFORNIA. *Featuring abundant color photographs, this lavish book relates the history of the missions; it includes details of how the missions were rebuilt after earthquakes and provides striking views.* (Teacher's resource.)

Compiled with the assistance of librarians Kathy Nicholson and Ann Ostenso (Monterey Peninsula Unified School District).

CALIFORNIA HERITAGE FIESTA

🔔 All-Californian Fiesta

🔔 Fiesta Fun

🔔 Mission Chain Bingo

To the Spanish who built California's missions and pueblos, a fiesta was a celebration of community and traditions. So what should a fiesta be like for today's multicultural, multicolored, multilingual California? Why, an All-Californian Fiesta, of course—with food, music, games, and fun from around the world (or around the block).

As a follow-up to your exploration of the Mission Period, have your students stage a modern-day fiesta celebrating the diverse heritage of the Golden State. Encourage them to contribute ideas based on their own ethnic heritage, or on research into the customs and traditions of other groups. By exploring California's diversity, they can learn that all Californians—not just the Spanish pioneers they study in history books—continue to play a historic role in creating our common culture.

*Besides suggestions to get them started, the handout pages in **All-Californian Fiesta** and **Fiesta Fun** provide tips on working together in teams—an increasingly important skill in our diverse society. As part of the festivities—or on its own—**Mission Chain Bingo** provides an exciting game based on mission facts and lore. Your students won't even notice how much they're learning!*

Teacher's Notes

Use this space to record your own notes about this section of activities.

All-Californian Fiesta

To California's Spanish settlers, a fiesta meant food, music, dance, and games. Most of all, a fiesta was a celebration of the community's heritage and traditions.

Unlike Mission days, today Californians represent cultures from all over the world—so a modern-day fiesta has many traditions to celebrate! Honor our state's diverse heritage by planning an <u>All-Californian</u> Fiesta. (Teacher: The ideas in **Fiesta Fun,** pages 25-29, may help.) Because an event like this takes cooperation and teamwork, here are tips for working together to plan your special day.

Planning Your All-Californian Fiesta

1. As a class, decide on different categories of things to include in your fiesta, such as Decorations, Food, Music and Dance, Skits, and Games. Include activities based on the traditions of a variety of cultural and ethnic groups, beginning with those represented in your class.

2. Divide the class into teams, one team per category. Each team has the following five tasks:

a. Brainstorm specific ideas for the category (for instance, the Food team brainstorms what kind of food to prepare and serve). Try using a Talking Feather (see box) when you're brainstorming.

b. Choose the ideas that are the most fun and the most practical. These are your team's *goals*.

c. Decide what specific steps must be taken to accomplish each goal. For instance, if the Food team decides to serve quesadillas (a Mexican dish), the steps might include (1) finding a recipe, (2) shopping for ingredients, (3) providing plates and forks, (4) cooking, (5) serving, and (6) cleaning up.

d. Divide up responsibility for the steps among the team members. If the team needs help to accomplish certain steps, you may need to ask for the class's cooperation. Be prepared to rethink an idea if the class is unable to provide the needed help.

e. Report the team's decisions to the class.

3. As a class, discuss the reports of each team and make any necessary adjustments to the overall fiesta plan.

The Talking Feather

Have you ever been in a group where everyone tries to talk at once, or a few people do all the talking? When this happens, try borrowing an idea from Native American culture--the Talking Feather.

A Talking Feather can be a real feather or one you make from colored paper. Only the person holding the Talking Feather is allowed to speak, while everyone else in the group listens. When the speaker is finished, the Talking Feather goes to the next person, who either speaks or passes the Feather on. Continue in this way until everyone has had enough chances to speak.

Tips for Teams

Many businesses in the United States use cooperative teams in their work. They have discovered that working in teams takes some special skills. Here are some ideas for making your own teamwork more successful.

1. Within each team, appoint a Captain, a Recorder, and a Reporter. Besides taking part in the team's discussions, these team members have special jobs:

☆ The Captain keeps the discussion focused on the task and makes sure that everyone gets a chance to speak.

☆ The Recorder writes down the team's ideas and decisions.

☆ The Reporter presents the results of the team's work orally to the class.

2. The remaining team members are just as important as the Captain, the Recorder, and the Reporter. All team members share responsibility for cooperating and respecting one another's ideas.

3. Whenever you use brainstorming to come up with creative ideas, follow these 4 simple rules:

☆ **Rule 1:** There are *no* "bad" ideas. Let people suggest whatever they think of, even if the ideas seem far-fetched! That's how you get creative ideas.

☆ **Rule 2:** Take turns quickly giving one idea at a time. A person always has the right to pass until the next turn.

☆ **Rule 3:** Have the Recorder write down every idea that is mentioned.

☆ **Rule 4:** Don't criticize or discuss any of the ideas until you are finished brainstorming. *After* you're done brainstorming, discuss each idea and select the best ones.

4. The Recorder can use the Planning Arrow (described below) to record the team's decisions. Post the Planning Arrows from all the teams in the classroom to remind everyone of their responsibilities.

The Planning Arrow: Aiming at a Goal

When you're working in teams to achieve a goal, a Planning Arrow can show what everyone is supposed to do. Here's how to make one:

1. On a sheet of paper, draw the shaft and arrowhead of the arrow.

2. To the right of the arrowhead, write down the group's goal (the "target").

3. On one side of the shaft, draw and label a "feather" (a diagonal line) for each step involved in reaching the goal. On the other side, draw and label a feather showing who is responsible for that step. (See illustration.)

4. Post the Planning Arrow where everyone in the team can see it. If you all do your part, you'll fly to your goal!

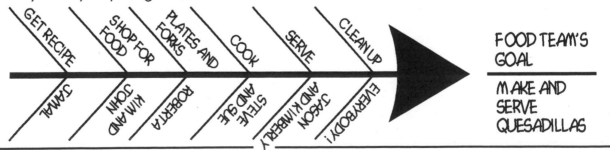

⌂ Cooperative
  learning
⌂ Art
⌂ Music
⌂ Performing arts
⌂ Math skills

Fiesta Fun

Your All-Californian Fiesta can be whatever you make it, as long as you make it fun! Brainstorm different cultures and ethnic groups to honor in the fiesta. The following pages contain ideas to get you started, but don't be shy about coming up with your own!

Decorations

Deck out the classroom with artwork and other decorations you can make or buy. Here are just a few ideas:

- ❖ Pinatas
- ❖ Banners
- ❖ Streamers
- ❖ Posters
- ❖ Murals

- ❖ Baskets
- ❖ Flowers
- ❖ Balloons
- ❖ Flags
- ❖ Place mats or name cards

Give your decorations a multicultural flavor. For instance, you could make travel posters showing scenes from some of the home countries of California's people. (You might be able to get actual posters from local travel agencies, or decorate homemade posters with pictures from magazines or travel brochures.) You can also borrow ideas from the Mission Indians and padres by using mission designs or murals in your decoration plan.

Bells on the El Camino

Here's an idea for a fiesta decoration with a mission theme. For many years, historical markers in the shape of mission bells told travelers on the El Camino that a mission was nearby. For your fiesta, create your own "historical markers" honoring the contributions of California's ethnic groups. Each student can contribute a bell by doing the following:

1. Draw and cut out a mission bell from construction paper, light cardboard, or other material.

2. Decorate one side of the bell with a design or other artwork honoring a person, event, or contribution connected with an ethnic group. The group does not have to be your own. (See illustration for an example.)

3. On the other side of the bell, write your name along with a few facts about the achievement or person you are honoring.

4. For a festive decoration, punch a small hole near the top of each bell and hang the bells on strings above the room. (You can also pin or tape the bells to the classroom walls or bulletin boards.)

Food and Drink

Finger-lickin' fiesta food can be one of the highlights of your celebration. You can have a "smorgasbord" (a Swedish word meaning a "variety"), with several kinds of ethnic foods. Or you can have a single ethnic theme, such as California Indian food, Mexican food, soul food, or Chinese food.

Research the origins of the foods you prepare and serve. Prepare a menu that tells about the history of your fiesta foods.

Song and Dance

A fiesta just wouldn't be the same without music and dance. Try learning and performing folk songs or dances from one or more cultures. See whether you can create traditional costumes to perform in. Tell the audience some of the background of the pieces you perform, such as where they came from and whether they originally celebrated special occasions.

You might also find recorded folk music to play during the fiesta. (Try your school or public library. Many libraries have recordings as well as books on song and dance.)

Make Mexican Chocolate

Chocolate was a favorite drink of the mission padres, and it is still a favorite in Mexico and many parts of Latin America. Here is a recipe for making the kind of hot chocolate the padres enjoyed:

Ingredients for 4 servings:

6 teaspoons grated chocolate
6 teaspoons granulated sugar
1 cup boiling water
3 cups scalded milk
nutmeg
cinnamon
1 teaspoon vanilla
2 eggs, well beaten

To Prepare

Mix the chocolate and sugar. Stir in the boiling water to dissolve the mixture. Cook for 5 minutes. Blend in the scalded milk, and cook over medium heat until hot. Add in the beaten eggs, plus a dash of cinnamon and nutmeg. Beat with a wire whip or egg beater until the chocolate is frothy.

Can You Find Out . . .

* What plant chocolate comes from?
* Where in the world the plant grows?
* Where cinnamon comes from?
* Where nutmeg comes from?

As you'll discover, Mexican chocolate is a truly international drink!

Adapted from *The Californians* (March/April 1992).

Skits

Stage a skit or two based on a mission theme, an event in California history, or a story about Californians from different cultures. (Teacher: See Readers' Theatre section, pages 47-56, for suggestions on creating original scripts based on stories and historical events.)

Games

Sports and games are part of every culture. Research one or more games to play that your classmates don't already know. Present some information to the class about the origins of the game (what culture it comes from, how it was played, and so on), and teach your classmates how to play.

Did You Know That . . .

☆ Board games (like checkers, chess, or gambling games) have been played by people in almost every culture in the world? (Two exceptions are Eskimos and Australian Aborigines.)

☆ In many cultures, games and sports began as religious rituals?

☆ The oldest surviving game board in the world (from ancient Egypt) is nearly 6,000 years old?

☆ During the Mission Period, two California Indians kicked a ball 100 miles in two days, from San Luis Obispo to San Juan Bautista?

☆ The game we know as chess is thousands of years old and was first played in ancient India?

To give you a head start, the Pomo Gambling Game (next page) is a variation of a game played by California Indians. It might seem to be purely a game of luck, but like most gambling games, it is based on mathematical ideas having to do with chance, or probability. You can investigate these ideas by trying the following: After playing for a while, record the results of 20 or more drops. Which result happens most often? Which happens least often?

If you play long enough, the 3-up, 3-down result should happen the most, and the 6-up and 6-down results should happen the least. Can you figure out why?

Teacher's Note: Another game to play is Mission Chain Bingo (page 34).

Pomo Gambling Game

This game is designed for 3-5 players. To play the game, prepare the "staves" (tongue depressors or Popsicle sticks) by decorating each stave on one side only.

Materials

6 staves, decorated on 1 side
1 betting chart for each player (see below)
1 marker for each player (button, coin, M&M, etc.)
1 tally sheet (see below)

How to Play

1. The players take turns dropping the 6 staves on the ground. Count how many land with the decorated side up.
2. Before each drop, all players place a marker on their betting charts to show what they guess the result will be. It is OK for different players to choose the same bet.
3. After each drop, score a "win" on the tally sheet for each player who made the correct guess. You may want to record the results of each drop on your betting chart to help you make guesses about future drops.
4. The player with the most wins after 5 rounds of play is the winner.

BETTING CHART — Place a marker on your guess:	Number of times this result occurs:
6 UP, 0 DOWN	
5 UP, 1 DOWN	
4 UP, 2 DOWN	
3 UP, 3 DOWN	
2 UP, 4 DOWN	
1 UP, 5 DOWN	
0 UP, 6 DOWN	

TALLY SHEET	
Player (name):	Wins:

Californians on Parade

Parades are often a highlight of fiestas and other special events. Your All-Californian Fiesta makes a great theme for a parade in which the marchers represent different cultural and ethnic groups. Here are three suggestions for using the idea of a parade to cap off your All-Californian Fiesta.

Idea #1: Have a Parade

As a class, plan a parade you can stage at your school. Ask school officials whether you can march through the school, so other classes can enjoy the show!

A parade can involve banners, balloons, and other decorations; costumes; music and songs; homemade drums and other noisemakers; dancing; and even "floats"! You might work in teams, with each team taking the part of a particular ethnic group. Make and decorate a banner or sign showing the group you are honoring.

Idea #2: Make a Parade Mural

A parade is an ideal theme for a butcher-paper mural in your classroom or school hallway. The background might be a California mission, while the foreground shows marchers from many groups and periods of California history, along with floats, animals, and other things you can draw. Note: Each student can create his or her own illustrations, cut them out, and pin or glue them onto the mural. That's easier than drawing directly on the mural, and you can also rearrange the parts of the parade.

Idea #3: Make a "TV Video" of Californians on Parade

Teams or individual students can create homemade "TV videos" of an All-Californian Parade by making a "video box" (see below). Have "announcers" describe and comment on the parade!

Make a "TV Video"

With a cardboard box, a roll of white shelf paper, and a couple of rollers (sticks or cardboard cylinders), you can make a "video box" that's perfect for showing marchers on parade.

1. Cut out a viewing area in the front of the box. The size of the area should fit the dimensions of your shelf paper.
2. Make rollers a little taller than the box. Cut holes in the top of the box for the rollers.
3. Draw and color the parade on the roll of shelf paper. Fasten one end of the roll to one roller with glue or tape. Fasten the other end to the second roller. Insert the "video" in the box through the viewing opening, and position the rollers so they stand straight up. Turn the rollers to create a moving picture of your parade.

CALIFORNIANS ON PARADE

Mission Chain *BINGO*

FREE				FREE
FREE				FREE

Write the names of the 21 California missions in the 21 empty squares. Mix up the names by writing them in a random order.

Mission Chain Bingo

Teacher's Page _____

Here's an exciting game to play as part of your Fiesta fun—or as a "rainy day" activity any time. It reinforces mission facts and develops skill in using the Mission Facts Table.

In Mission Chain Bingo, the squares on the game cards show the names of the 21 missions, plus 4 free squares. Instead of calling out "Bingo numbers," you will call out clues that the players must figure out within a limited time to know which squares they can cover. The first player to complete a Mission Chain by covering one complete row of squares (vertically, horizontally, or diagonally) is the winner.

Preparation

1. Create the clue cards (see next page).
2. To create a unique game card for each player, photocopy the facing page, and distribute one copy to each student. Each student should write short versions of the names of the 21 missions (e.g., "Soledad") in the 21 empty squares. Important: Advise students to mix up the mission names by filling in the squares randomly, so that no two cards are exactly alike. They can work from their Mission Facts tables, checking off each name as they write it, so that they don't write the same name twice.
3. To play the game, each player will need a copy of the Mission Facts Table and 15 or so "markers"—small objects such as bits of colored paper or cardboard, lima beans, or pennies. For extra fun, use edible markers like jelly beans or M&M's. Then the players can eat them when the game is over!
4. You might want to have small prizes for the winners (you can play the game several times).

MISSION SAN DIEGO

Playing the Game

1. Shuffle the clue cards. Read one clue from the first card. Allow the players 30 seconds or so to figure out which mission is being named, whether from memory or by referring to the Mission Facts Table. Caution the players not to say the answer out loud.
2. Set aside the clue card so that you will be able to verify which missions have been "called."
3. Whenever you call out a "Free" card, each player can cover any *one* corner ("Free") square.
4. Continue reading clues, one card at a time, until a player completes a Mission Chain and calls out "Bingo!"
5. To verify a "win," have the player read the names of the covered missions and compare them with the clue cards you have set aside. If there are any errors, the player is disqualified for that round, and play continues.
6. To play again, reshuffle the clue cards. You can read different clues every time you play. If some clues are read in more than one game, don't worry—students who learn their mission facts by heart will be rewarded by knowing the answer! You might also have students exchange game cards for each new game.

Mission Chain Bingo Clue Cards

Teacher: Photocopy this page. For easier handling, cut and mount on 3" x 5" index cards (one mission per card). Create 3 "Free" cards and shuffle between the mission cards.

SAN DIEGO
1. Alta California's 1st mission
2. Burned in 1775
3. Named for St. Didacus of Alcala

SAN CARLOS
1. Located near present-day Carmel
2. Fewest mission Indians in 1832
3. Serra's headquarters

SAN ANTONIO
1. Named for St. Anthony of Padua
2. Near present-day Jolon
3. Noted for fine horses

SAN GABRIEL
1. Most crops in 1832
2. Founded by Padres Cambon and Somera
3. 2nd in livestock in 1832

SAN LUIS OBISPO
1. Founded 1 year after San Gabriel
2. Named for a bishop
3. About 300 miles from Mission San Diego

SAN FRANCISCO
1. Popular name means "sorrows"
2. Founded by Francisco Palou
3. 2nd fewest mission Indians in 1832

SAN JUAN CAPISTRANO
1. 2nd mission founded in 1776
2. 900 mission Indians in 1832
3. Famous for its faithful birds

SANTA CLARA
1. Named for a female saint of Assisi
2. Today part of a university campus
3. Founded by Padres de la Pena and Murguia

SAN BUENAVENTURA
1. In present-day Ventura
2. Name means "Good Fortune"
3. Serra's last mission

SANTA BARBARA
1. Lasuen's 1st mission
2. Founded 4 years after Buenaventura
3. "Queen of the Missions"

LA PURISIMA
1. 372 mission Indians in 1832
2. Near present-day Lompoc
3. Scene of Indian revolt in 1824

SAN FRANCISCO DE SOLANO
1. Fewest livestock in 1832
2. Founded on 4th of July
3. Farthest mission from San Diego

SANTA CRUZ
1. Fewest crops in 1832
2. Looted by townspeople in 1818
3. Name means "Holy Cross"

SOLEDAD
1. Scene of epidemic in 1802
2. Named for "Our Lady of Solitude"
3. 2nd mission founded in 1791

SAN JOSE
1. Known during Gold Rush as "Mission St. Joe"
2. 1st of 4 missions founded in 1797
3. Second most crops in 1832

SAN JUAN BAUTISTA
1. Founded same month as San Jose
2. Named for John the Baptist
3. Famous for Indian choir

SAN MIGUEL
1. 10 fewer mission Indians than Buenaventura in 1832
2. Founded 1 month after San Juan Bautista
3. Scene of murder in 1849

SAN FERNANDO REY
1. Scene of mini gold rush in 1843
2. 1st mission named for a king
3. About 130 miles from Mission San Diego

SAN LUIS REY
1. Named for a king of France
2. Most livestock in 1832
3. Closest mission to Mission San Diego

SANTA INES
1. Famous for saddles
2. Near present-day Solvang
3. Founded by Estevan Tapis

SAN RAFAEL
1. Originally a hospital
2. Founded by Vicente Sarria
3. Next-to-last mission to be founded

 FREE

TALES OF TREASURE

♤ Time Travel Treasure Hunt

♤ Un-Buried Treasures

♤ My Special Treasure

One of the lessons of **Tales and Treasures of California's Missions** is that many things are "treasures" besides silver and gold. The memories preserved in colorful tales of long ago, aged cemeteries, and the missions themselves are all genuine treasures to cherish and protect.

In this section students explore the many meanings of "treasure." **Time Travel Treasure Hunt** sends them on a journey into the past to trade a contemporary treasure for an artifact from mission days. **Un-Buried Treasures** encourages them to seek out and celebrate the special objects, places, and people in their present-day community. And in **My Special Treasure** they share their feelings about a favorite person or thing in their own lives. Creativity, critical thinking, self-esteem, and personal expression are the real "treasures" in this set of activities.

Teacher's Notes

Use this space to record your own notes about this section of activities.

Time Travel Treasure Hunt

21ST CENTURY TIME TRAVEL, INC.

Attention, Time Traveler!

You have been chosen by historians for a very special task. You are about to ride in a Time Machine through the centuries to California's mission days. Enter your destination (the mission and the year) into the machine, and presto! The next thing you know, you will be standing in the mission garden, looking at a very surprised Padre Junipero Serra, or a Mission Indian!

Warning! Battery life in the Time Machine is strictly limited. We strongly suggest that you return within two hours, or you may be stuck in the past forever.

You have two important jobs on your journey. (1) Record your observations of mission life in words and drawings. (2) Bring something back with you to the present--some treasure from the past (called an artifact) that can help us understand how people lived in those long-ago times.

Good luck--and don't forget to come back before the batteries run down. We don't want to be reading about you in our history books!

Directions

1. Choose a California mission and a year for your journey—for instance, "Mission San Carlos, 1775." (Your teacher may assign your destination.)

2. To obtain an artifact from the padres or Indians, you must trade for it. (You don't expect those people to just give you one of their treasures, do you?) Therefore, choose a modern-day "treasure" to bring with you that you can trade for an artifact. Select an object that would be interesting or useful to people of mission days. (Why wouldn't a TV be a good idea?)

3. Make your journey through time in your imagination. (Looking at books on the missions and California Indians may help.) Be observant—what scenes do you see? Who do you meet? What object would make a good artifact to bring back?

4. Make or find an artifact to bring home with you. For instance, you could make a silver mission cross with two sticks or rulers, some tape, and some aluminum foil. What other objects used by the Indians or padres could you find or make?

5. Record your adventure on your personal Time Travel Log.

6. Tell the class about your trip, and share your artifact. What does the artifact tell us about life in mission days?

Teacher's Note: See instructions on page 40.

Teacher's Instructions Page

A. In Advance

1. Optional: Enrich this activity by preparing Time Travel Passports for each student (see opposite page).

a. Make photocopies of the passport page. Follow cutting and folding instructions in the box below.

b. While you can have students choose their own missions and years to visit, you may want to specify missions and years to ensure a good selection. To do so, fill in the "Place" and "Year" on the Passports. Fill in the "Expires" blank to indicate the due date.

c. To make assignments to individual students, fill in the "Name" as well. Or you can leave the "Name" blank and distribute the Passports at random. (You can add some excitement by letting students draw their Passports from a Treasure Box to discover their destinations.)

d. Have students fill in the rest of the Passport. Explain that the blank space on the left inside page is for a "passport photo." Students can paste in a wallet-sized photo or draw a self-portrait.

2. Photocopy and distribute the Time Travel Treasure Hunt activity page and the Time Travel Log (page 42).

B. Discussion and Activity

1. To prepare students for their journey through time, discuss the following concepts: (a) *Time travel:* What would it be like to travel through time? What problems would a 20th-century traveler face when visiting mission days? (b) *Passports:* What are passports used for, and why? (c) *Communication:* How will your time travelers communicate with padres and California Indians who do not share their language? (Your Spanish-speaking students may have an advantage here.) Point out that the people on the frontier faced exactly this problem. How did the Indians, Spanish, and English-speaking sailors and visitors teach one another their languages? (d) *Trade and barter:* Point out that trade and barter were important economic activities in

mission times. What kinds of contemporary objects would make a good trade for an artifact? What *wouldn't* be any use to people of mission days? Why? (e) *Artifacts:* How can objects from the past tell us what life was like? What objects would make good artifacts from mission days?

2. Encourage students to do research in order to vividly imagine their journeys. What do they see, hear, smell, touch, taste? Allow several days for students to do their research and create their Time Travel Logs and artifacts.

C. Extensions

1. Have students each draw pictures of their Time Machine. What kinds of dials and instruments does it have?

2. Have students write a first-person news story about their journey through time.

3. Create a class display of the Time Travel Logs, Passports, and artifacts. Invite guests to view your own historical museum.

4. Have students do pantomime skits to show how they "talked" to the padres or Indians they met. How did they explain what their modern treasure was good for?

5. As a class or in small groups, have students brainstorm ideas for artifacts of life today that would be interesting to historians 200 years from now. Suppose they could pack a time capsule (say, one that was about as big as a closet). What would they put in it for future historians to find? Why?

Folding Instructions for Time Travel Passport (page 41)

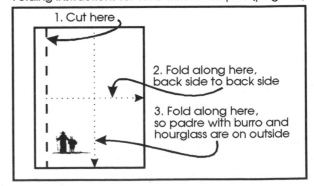

1. Cut here

2. Fold along here, back side to back side

3. Fold along here, so padre with burro and hourglass are on outside

Name: _____

Date of
birth: _____

Country of
citizenship: _____

Century of
citizenship: _____

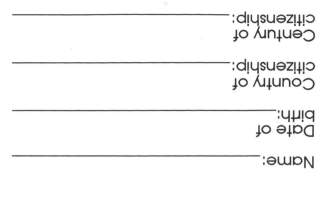

Expires: _____
(date assignment due)

_____
(year)

in the year

_____
(place)

*This passport entitles
the bearer to travel
through time to*

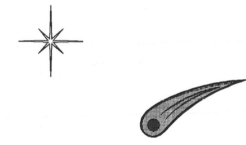

Time Travel
Passport

*United States
of America*

_____ **'s Time Travel Log**

(your name)

1. Where did you go?

_____

_____

_____

Draw a star on the map to show where you went

2. What year was it? _____

3. What did you see?

_____

_____

_____

_____

_____

4. Who did you meet?

_____

_____

5. What treasure did you take with you?

_____

_____

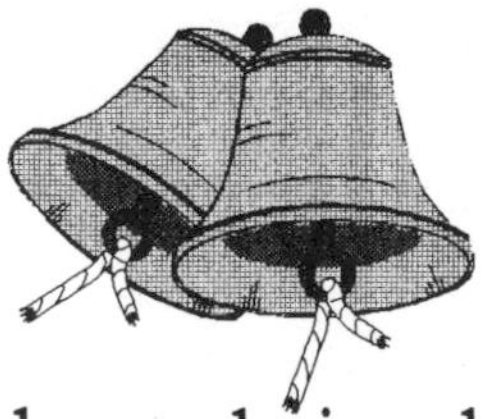

6. What treasure did you bring back?

_____

_____

♧ Local history
♧ Observation
♧ Critical thinking
♧ Art
♧ Writing

Un-Buried Treasures

We all love tales of buried treasure, but some treasures are out in the open for all to see. Some un-buried treasures are old, like an original mission church. Some are new, like an exciting airport terminal. Some are big, like Disneyland. Some are small, like a tiny aquarium of exotic fish in a pet store or restaurant.

What un-buried treasures are there in your community? Do you have a favorite place to go, or sight to see? What special object, place, or person helps to make your town or city interesting and exciting? Maybe it's something (or someone) you've seen every day, but never noticed before. Remember, a treasure is anything that is special—even if it's special just to you.

Golden Gate Bridge

Directions _____

1. Choose a treasure in your community to find out about and share. See whether you can find out some facts about it. Where is it? Who does it belong to? Where did it come from? How old is it? What makes it special?

2. Make a drawing of your treasure. (Teacher: Photocopy following page.) Include a small map that tells where people can find it. Choose a landmark or street that people will recognize, and show where the treasure is. You can see an example on this page.

Extensions _____

1. Make a display by mounting your Un-Buried Treasures sheets on poster board. Write to the mayor, a local librarian, or other official describing your class project. See whether you can display your Un-Buried Treasures at City Hall, the city library, a bank, coffee house, or some other public place.

2. Write to the local newspaper describing your project. The newspaper may want to do a story—complete with photos!

3. Use your Un-Buried Treasures sheets to make a guide book of your community's special places. You can even create your own personal "tour of the town." Going to see all the treasures would make a great field trip!

Un-Buried Treasures of _____

(your community)

_____

(name of treasure)

_____

_____

_____

_____

by _____

(your name)

My Special Treasure

Do you have a special treasure? Treasures don't have to be made of gold and silver. A treasure is anything that is special to you—something you are very glad to have, and that you would be very sorry to lose.

What is your favorite treasure? Maybe it's a thing, like a toy or souvenir. Maybe it's a place, like a secret hideout or place to play. Maybe it's a pet. Or maybe it's a person, like a parent or grandparent, a brother or sister, or a special friend.

Whatever your special treasure is, it's something to celebrate. Here are some ideas for sharing your treasure with the class.

Directions

1. Choose the treasure you want to share. Write a poem about it that tells how you feel about it or why it is special.

2. Make a Treasure Box for your treasure. A gift box, shoe box, or other container can be decorated with paints, crayons, shelf paper, or construction paper. For small treasures, your teacher may give you a do-it-yourself box to make. (Teacher: Photocopy next page.) If your treasure is too big for a box, put something in the box that can "stand for" your treasure—perhaps a drawing, a photograph, or an object connected with your treasure.

3. Bring your poem and Treasure Box (with your treasure inside) to class.

4. Take turns presenting your treasures to the class. Before you open your box or tell what your treasure is, play Twenty Questions. See whether the class can guess what your treasure is by asking up to 20 questions that can be answered "yes" or "no." (Examples: Is it bigger than a shoe box? Is it alive?)

5. When someone guesses your treasure (or the 20 questions are used up), open your box and show what's inside. Read your poem out loud.

6. Make a class display of your treasures and poems. Invite your parents or other guests to come and see the display.

7. Your may want to learn and sing the song "My Favorite Things" from the musical *The Sound of Music*, by Oscar Hammerstein II and Richard Rodgers.

How to Make a Treasure Box

1. Turn the page upside down and write your name before the " 's " on the front of your treasure box. You may color your treasure box if you wish.

2. Cut just outside of the dark outer line all the way around the box.

3. Fold along the dashed lines.

4. Glue or tape the tabs to the inside of the front and back of the box.

5. Fold down the shaded tab attatched to the top of the box and tuck it inside to close your box.

6. Now you are ready to put your special treasure in your box!

TOP

BACK

TAB

TAB

BOTTOM

TAB

TAB

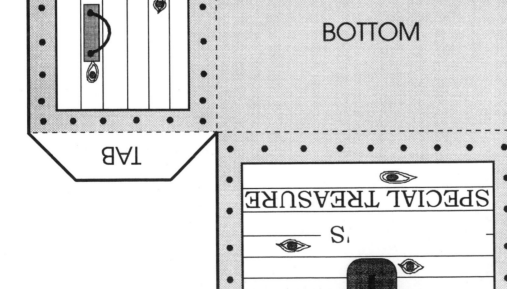

SPECIAL TREASURE

'S

FRONT

READERS' THEATRE _____

 ♫ Do-It-Yourself Readers' Theatre

 ♫ "The Faith of Padre Serra"

You've probably already discovered Readers' Theatre as an exciting way to involve students in their reading. Although you can look for ready-made scripts (or prepare one yourself), another way to generate scripts is to teach students how to make their own.

To create their own scripts, students will need to vividly imagine the characters' world, including their motivations. They can also learn basic concepts such as character, conflict, climax, and resolution—concepts that provide a framework for deepening their appreciation of both stories and historical incidents.

This section's **Do-It-Yourself Readers' Theatre** introduces these ideas by means of an incident related in **Tales and Treasures of California's Missions.** The sample adaptation, **"The Faith of Padre Serra,"** illustrates this lesson, but it can also be produced on its own.

Try dividing the class into cooperative groups that brainstorm, create, and produce their own Readers' Theatre skits. The skits can be presented as part of the festivities in your All-Californian Fiesta!

Five P's for Polished Performances

In **Do-It-Yourself Readers' Theatre,** students learn five "**P**'s" for adapting a story into a script. Here are five more "**P**'s" you can use to coach students in effective oral delivery—whether of speeches, reports, or plays.

☆ **Posture:** Stand up straight and tall. Hold the script or other material away from your face. Look at the audience.

☆ **Pause:** When you arrive "on stage," pause a moment and quietly take a deep breath. That will help you relax, and you'll take command of the audience's attention.

☆ **Projection:** Speak loudly and distinctly, so everyone can hear. "Throw" your voice all the way to the back row; don't talk to the people in the front of the room.

☆ **Poise:** Don't let audience giggles or other distractions interfere with your delivery. Calmly pause and wait until you have the audience's attention. Stay in character.

☆ **Pride:** Be proud of your courage in getting up to speak. When you're done, smile (don't laugh). **P**ause a moment before exiting, and walk tall. Keep your **p**oise and **p**osture until you are completely offstage.

♨ Analytical skills
♨ Literature
   appreciation
♨ Creative writing
♨ Oral interpretation
♨ Cooperative
   learning

Do-It-Yourself Readers' Theatre

A great way to share exciting stories is to turn them into Readers' Theatre skits. These skits are short plays that you and your friends can present to the rest of the class. In Readers' Theatre skits (unlike some other kinds of plays), the actors read from a script instead of memorizing their lines.

You can find material for Readers' Theatre in stories, fables, or historical episodes. We'll use an example of a historical incident to show how to create your own script for a Readers' Theatre skit.

The incident is described in the Mission San Diego chapter of **Tales and Treasures of California's Missions.** Here is a short version of the story.

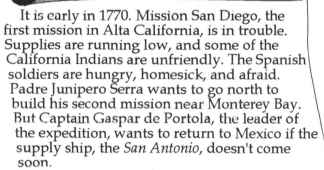

It is early in 1770. Mission San Diego, the first mission in Alta California, is in trouble. Supplies are running low, and some of the California Indians are unfriendly. The Spanish soldiers are hungry, homesick, and afraid. Padre Junipero Serra wants to go north to build his second mission near Monterey Bay. But Captain Gaspar de Portola, the leader of the expedition, wants to return to Mexico if the supply ship, the *San Antonio*, doesn't come soon.

Serra begs Portola to wait nine days, until St. Joseph's Day, before giving up. On St. Joseph's Day, the men spot a sail on the horizon, but the ship sails on into the mist. Serra again asks Portola to wait a few days longer. Perhaps the ship is lost!

Four days later, the *San Antonio* arrives at San Diego. The ship captain had gone up the coast looking for Portola! But then the captain turned back because the ship needed repairs. The supplies arrive just in time. Thanks to Serra's faith that the ship would come, the expedition can go on. Portola agrees to set out for Monterey, and Padre Serra's mission chain is saved.

This story is interesting, but it isn't yet a play. Let's see how we can turn it (or any story) into a script for Readers' Theatre.

Adapting a Story for Readers' Theatre

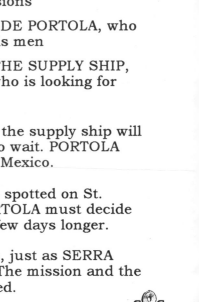

Here are **5 "P's"** for adapting (changing) a story for Readers' Theatre: **P**ick, **P**lot, **P**repare, **P**ractice, and **P**resent.

PICK a Story

1. For a good dramatic skit, PICK a story that has four main elements: <u>Characters</u>, <u>Conflict</u>, <u>Climax</u>, and <u>Resolution</u>. To see what these words mean, let's use our example story of Serra and Portola.

Story Element	Example
a. <u>Characters</u> are people (or, sometimes, animals or even supernatural beings). Interesting characters have their own special ways of acting and talking. Most important, they have their own *motives*, or reasons for doing things.	**a.** PADRE JUNIPERO SERRA, who is eager to build missions CAPTAIN GASPAR DE PORTOLA, who is worried about his men The CAPTAIN OF THE SUPPLY SHIP, the *San Antonio*, who is looking for Portola
b. The <u>Conflict</u> is a problem or disagreement that the characters must do something about.	**b.** SERRA believes the supply ship will come, and wants to wait. PORTOLA wants to return to Mexico.
c. The <u>Climax</u> of a story is the moment when the characters must take action to solve the conflict, for better or worse.	**c.** When the sail is spotted on St. Joseph's Day, PORTOLA must decide whether to wait a few days longer.
d. The <u>Resolution</u> is the way the problem gets solved, and what happens to the characters as a result.	**d.** The ship arrives, just as SERRA believed it would. The mission and the expedition are saved.

2. You can use the Readers' Theatre Planning Sheet to help you identify these elements of a story or historical episode. (Teacher: See page 52.)

PLOT the Skit

The next step is to PLOT the scenes and actions that will tell the story.

1. Decide how many scenes you will need. Some stories can be told in one scene. You only need separate scenes if some time goes by in between parts of the story. In our story, we might choose three scenes because time passes between the important events.

a. Scene 1: Introduces the main Characters and the Conflict (should they wait for the ship?).

b. Scene 2: The ship is spotted on St. Joseph's Day, and Portola must decide what to do (the Climax).

c. Scene 3: The ship finally arrives (the Resolution).

continued...

2. You might decide to have one or more Narrators who can introduce the situation at the start of the skit. The Narrators can also provide any necessary explanations between scenes.

PREPARE the Script

Plays and skits tell their stories through *dialogue* (speeches made by the characters). PREPARE a *script* that contains all the dialogue, plus any speeches made by Narrators.

1. If the story you are using already has dialogue, you have a head start on making a script! Just cross out words like "she said" and "he said," and let the actors read the words and sentences that are inside quotation marks. You can leave out other information that the audience doesn't need. You can also change some of the speeches to include important information, or you can put information in speeches made by Narrators.

2. Some stories don't have enough dialogue already in them (or any dialogue at all, like the one we are using). In this case you have to make up the dialogue. To do so, think about how the characters feel about their situation, and imagine how they might talk. For instance, here's a bit of dialogue for Serra and Portola that shows their conflict:

> PORTOLA: It is time we prepared to return to Mexico—while we still can.

> SERRA: No, Captain! If we lose faith now, the mission will fail.

3. Try to put the most important parts of the story in the dialogue, rather than in words spoken by Narrators. That will make your story dramatic and exciting. You may need to invent characters for this purpose. For instance, in our story, we might include a couple of Portola's soldiers to show how the men were hungry and afraid.

PRACTICE!

When your script is ready, do what professional actors do—PRACTICE! In your practices (called *rehearsals*), read slowly and with expression, in a way that shows what the character is feeling. Learn at least some of the words in your part by heart. That way, you can look at the audience more. (By the way, face the audience—not the other actors!)

PRESENT the Skit

When you're ready for the big day, PRESENT your skit to an audience. Then take a bow and enjoy the applause!

Your teacher may give you a complete script to read that is based on the ideas we've described. It may give you ideas for writing your own Readers' Theatre scripts.

Readers' Theatre

Planning Sheet

Story or historical event: _____

Setting (time and place): _____

_____

_____

Characters:

     Name   Description

1. _____   _____

2. _____   _____

3. _____   _____

4. _____   _____

5. _____   _____

Problem or conflict: _____

_____

_____

_____

Climax: _____

_____

_____

_____

_____

_____

Resolution: _____

_____

_____

_____

_____

The Faith of Padre Serra

Adapted from ***Tales and Treasures of California's Missions***
by Randall A. Reinstedt

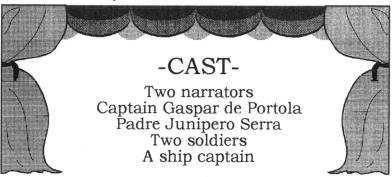

-CAST-

Two narrators
Captain Gaspar de Portola
Padre Junipero Serra
Two soldiers
A ship captain

Narrator 1:	The year is 1770—six years before the signing of the Declaration of Independence. The place is Mission San Diego, the first Spanish settlement in present-day California.
Narrator 2:	The Spanish have moved north from Mexico to establish new outposts. With them is Padre Junipero Serra. Serra's fondest hope is to found a number of missions. He wants to make friends with the native Californians, the Indians, and baptize them.
Narrator 1:	But Mission San Diego is in trouble. Many of the California Indians resent the Spanish invaders. Some of the Spanish are sick, and all of them are hungry.
Narrator 2:	The leader of the expedition, Captain Gaspar de Portola, summons Padre Serra to his headquarters. With him are two soldiers.
Serra:	You sent for me, Captain?
Portola:	Padre Serra, our situation is getting worse by the hour. I know how dearly you wish to go north and build your second mission near Monterey Bay. I know your deep desire to preach to the native people. But I fear the time is near when we cannot hold out any longer. These men can tell you.
Soldier 1:	The soldiers are hungry, Padre. And many are sick.
Soldier 2:	They are afraid of attacks by these Indians you love so much.
Soldier 1:	They don't want to die, Padre.
Soldier 2:	Especially not here—in this empty place! They want to return where men speak our language—

Soldier 1:	And where there is medicine for the sick.
Soldier 2:	And good Spanish food!
Serra:	I know how the men suffer. But we are on a great mission. It is the King's work. It is God's work! Surely, if we wait just a few days more, the supply ship will come—
Portola:	Ah, yes, the supply ship. The *phantom* supply ship, Padre! I am beginning to think there is no ship.
Soldier 1:	Perhaps it is lost, or shipwrecked.
Soldier 2:	Perhaps it will come only in time to bury us all!
Portola:	You see how it is, Padre. As the leader of this expedition, I must be responsible for these men. It is time we prepared to return to Mexico—while we still can.
Serra:	No, Captain! If we lose faith now, the mission will fail. Then no one will dare to come here again. God's work will never be done!
Soldier 1:	If God wants us to do this work, then God can send us a ship!
Soldier 2:	Or drop some bread and fresh water from the sky! That's what we need, Padre—a miracle.
Serra:	No—no miracle. Only a little faith. I beg you, Captain—wait a few days more. Look—St. Joseph's Day is just nine days away. That is a great and holy day. Wait until then, Captain. Surely we can hold out for nine days.
Portola:	You trouble me, Padre. All this talk of duty and faith! Very well. You shall have your nine days. But if the ship has not come by St. Joseph's Day, we return to Mexico!
Narrator 1:	For eight long days the Spanish watched the ocean, anxiously looking for the welcome sight of a sail.
Narrator 2:	While Serra prayed and begged the men to be brave, Portola paced and worried. Every day the supplies ran lower, and the men grumbled more.
Narrator 1:	At last St. Joseph's Day dawned. But still there was no sign of the supply ship.
Narrator 2:	Once again Portola called for Padre Serra.

Portola:	Well, Padre Serra, I have waited longer than I wished. Now St. Joseph's Day has arrived—but no ship! I have given orders to begin preparing for the return journey to Mexico.
Serra:	The day is young, Captain. The ship may still arrive.
Portola:	You are stubborn in your faith, Padre. I admire you for it. But I must make my decision on real things, not prayers. We need food, and medicine. We need hope. Padre, we leave for Mexico tomorrow.
Narrator 1:	Just then, excited voices are heard outside. At the lookout where the men have been watching the sea, soldiers are shouting.
Soldiers 1 & 2:	Look! A sail! A sail!
Narrator 2:	Portola and Serra run to the lookout point.
Portola:	A sail, you say? Where?
Soldier 1:	There, Captain—in the mist.
Serra:	I knew it would come.
Portola:	A sail it may be, but it's the sail of a phantom ship! I can barely make it out in the fog. Bah, it's just a trick of the light.
Soldier 2:	No, Captain. The mist has closed around it, but we saw it, clear as day. Well, nearly. It's the supply ship!
Portola:	Then why does it not turn this way? Why does it disappear into the fog, going north?
Soldier 1:	They might be lost. Oh, curse this fog!
Soldier 2:	Look, it's vanished. Maybe it is a phantom ship after all.
Serra:	Captain, it is no phantom. That is our ship. I know it. It has come on St. Joseph's Day.
Portola:	It has come—and gone, Padre. And it has taken our supplies with it.
Serra:	Perhaps they *are* lost, Captain. Please, wait a few days longer. They will find us. Now that we have seen the sail, we must have courage, and wait.
Narrator 1:	Impressed by Serra's faith, and the incident of the sail, Portola again agrees to wait a few days more.

Narrator 2:	Four days go by, and at last Serra's faith is rewarded.
Narrator 1:	Once again the cry "A sail!" goes up over the settlement. This time there is no doubt. The Spanish ship *San Antonio* has arrived with the badly needed supplies.
Narrator 2:	As soon as the *San Antonio* is safely in the harbor, the ship's captain is rushed to Portola's headquarters.
Portola:	Your ship is a most welcome sight, Captain. We had given up hope—well, except for Padre Serra here.
Serra:	But then we saw your sail on St. Joseph's Day. It *was* your sail, wasn't it?
Ship Captain:	It was. You see, my orders were to sail north and meet up with Captain Portola at Monterey. We only came back because we had trouble up the coast and needed repairs. I had no idea you were so desperate, or we would have brought the supplies here directly on St. Joseph's Day.
Serra:	You brought us something better than supplies, Captain. You brought us faith.
Ship Captain:	It's a strange sort of faith that grows stronger when your food passes you by!
Portola:	Never mind that now. The important thing is that the men will be fed and made well. And judging from the captain's orders, I believe I know what we must do next. It seems we are expected to be in the north. You shall have your second mission, Padre. And many more after that, God willing!
Serra:	Yes—many more. A chain of missions, Captain—strung like jewels on a string along the coast of Alta California!
Portola:	Soldier!
Soldier 2:	Yes, Captain?
Portola:	Cancel the order to prepare for the return to Mexico. Tell the men to eat well and to rest. They will need their strength.
Soldier 2:	And when they are fed and rested, what then?
Portola:	What then? Why, I believe Padre Serra might have an idea.
Serra:	To Monterey?
Portola:	Yes Padre. As soon as all is ready—we leave for Monterey!